WHO WE ARE AND
WHAT WE BELIEVE

KNOWING WHO WE ARE
The Wesleyan Way of Grace

Knowing Who We Are

978-1-7910-3203-6

978-1-7910-3202-9 eBook

Knowing Who We Are: Leader Guide

978-1-7910-3205-0

978-1-7910-3204-3 eBook

Knowing Who We Are: DVD

978-1-7910-3206-7

Who We Are and What We Believe:

50 Questions about The UMC

(a companion reader to the study)

978-1-7910-3208-1

978-1-7910-3207-4 eBook

Also by Laceye C. Warner

All the Good:

A Wesleyan Way of Christmas

The Method of Our Mission:

United Methodist Polity & Organization

Laceye C. Warner

WHO WE ARE AND WHAT WE BELIEVE

50 QUESTIONS ABOUT THE UMC

Abingdon Press | Nashville

Who We Are and What We Believe

50 Questions about The UMC

Copyright © 2024 Abingdon Press
All rights reserved.

Library of Congress Control Number: 2024935137

978-1-7910-3208-1

MANUFACTURED IN THE UNITED STATES OF AMERICA

CONTENTS

Who We Are

What We Believe

What We Do

A Sampling of Key Wesleyan Texts

WHO WE ARE

1. What does "Methodism" mean?

Methodism is a form of Protestant Christianity that began as a renewal movement within the Church of England in the eighteenth century. It was largely led by John Wesley and his brother Charles, along with other influential figures who nurtured and supported the movement.

The term "Methodism" or "Methodists" originated as a derisive term from those outside the movement, in reference to the systematic or methodical emphasis on religious devotion and discipline. For instance, John and Charles Wesley and other members of what was known as "the Holy Club" at Oxford used a cipher or code in their small journals that could fit into their coat pockets. The code allowed them to describe their activities throughout the day, sometimes every fifteen minutes, in a discreet way. Christian activities included reading Scripture, prayer, fasting, attending public worship, as well as visiting and caring for incarcerated, impoverished, and vulnerable persons.

In addition to tracking their practices throughout their days and weeks, they would evaluate their attitudes and responses to their Christian living using a list of questions. During the regular gatherings, participants would share their journals with one another seeking accountability, guidance, and encouragement.

Methodism began in Great Britain and eventually spread to America by the end of the eighteenth century. A number of Protestant denominations today trace their origins to the Methodist movement of John and Charles Wesley, including The United Methodist Church.

Hallmarks of Methodism include an emphasis on both personal piety and social action; meeting in small groups for spiritual growth; a theological emphasis on God's grace, as well as the idea of sanctification by which we continue to grow in grace; and a connectional structure that includes local, regional, and global conferences.

2. When and how did The United Methodist Church begin?

Though the United Methodist denomination itself began in 1968, with the merger of The Methodist Church and The Evangelical United Brethren Church, the origins of The United Methodist Church go further back. All Methodist denominations ultimately trace their origins to the Methodist movement led by John and Charles Wesley in the 1700s.

The Methodist movement emerged as a renewal movement within the Church of England in the eighteenth century. Different from many other Christian traditions, Methodism did not form as a protest in reaction to conflict over beliefs. The main characteristic of the Methodist movement is its missional nature.

All Wesleyan and Methodist Christians are connected to the lives and ministries of John Wesley (1703–1791) and his brother, Charles (1707–1788). Both John and Charles were Church of England priests who volunteered as missionaries to the colony of Georgia, arriving in March 1736. Their mission was far from an unqualified success, and both returned to England disillusioned and discouraged.

The Wesley brothers had transforming religious experiences in May 1738, under the influence of Moravian missionaries. John's experience on May 24 of that year at a Moravian meeting on Aldersgate Street, London, has a prominent place in The Methodist Church's memory. Shortly thereafter, both brothers began preaching a message of new birth and sanctification in Anglican religious societies and even outdoors. They also established missional and philanthropic enterprises to promote social change.

The goal of this movement was to "reform the nation, particularly the church; and to spread scriptural holiness over the land." Over time a pattern of organization and discipline emerged. It included a set of General Rules, societies made up of class meetings (small groups in which members of Methodist societies watched over one another), and band meetings (smaller confessional groups divided by gender), all connected by traveling lay preachers.

(Adapted from *The Book of Discipline,* "A Brief History of The United Methodist Church," p. 12)

3. Who was John Wesley?

John Wesley (1703–1791) was a priest in the Church of England and theologian who led the eighteenth-century Methodist renewal movement in England.

Wesley was known for an emphasis on piety and discipline in the Christian life; both his and his companions' rigorous, methodical approach to practicing their faith at Oxford led to the name "Methodist" as a derisive term. Wesley was also known for outdoor preaching to large crowds, as were other early Methodist leaders, and for bringing people together in classes or bands, organizational units through which individuals could experience growth in God's grace together. Wesley's organizational leadership is a key reason for the growth of early Methodism.

Theologically, Wesley's contributions include an emphasis on God's grace, especially the distinction between prevenient, justifying, and sanctifying grace; a via media or "middle way" that emphasized both faith and good works as well as social action and personal piety; and a practical approach to Christianity that prioritized a loving heart over correct beliefs.

Often regarded as the founder of Methodism, John Wesley's influence continues today in the many Methodist and Wesleyan denominations that trace their origins back to the Methodist movement.

4. Who was Charles Wesley?

Charles Wesley (1707–1788) was the younger brother of John Wesley who also played a vital role in the leadership and growth of the Methodist renewal movement in England.

Charles Wesley is most well known for the hymns he wrote. He wrote more than 6,500 hymns during his lifetime, many of which continue to be popular today in Methodist and non-Methodist churches alike. His most well-known hymns include "Hark! The Herald Angels Sing," "Christ the Lord Is Risen Today," and "Love Divine, All Loves Excelling."

Charles Wesley's hymns are vibrant expressions of his theology and spirituality and have played an important role in shaping Methodist theology and worship. Charles Wesley's hymns have taught and expressed the faith in countless Methodist churches.

While his leadership and impact were of a different character than that of his brother John, Charles Wesley undoubtedly made a lasting contribution to the formation and legacy of the eighteenth-century Methodist movement that continues today.

5. Who was Susanna Wesley?

Susanna Wesley (1669–1742) was the mother of John and Charles Wesley, who founded the Methodist renewal movement in the eighteenth century. She gave birth to nineteen children, although nine died in infancy. Susanna placed a high value on education and religion, and instilled these values in her children through teaching and spiritual discipline.

Susanna educated each of her children, including teaching the girls to read, even before they could sew, a highly unusual practice. She maintained close relationships through correspondence, including John and Charles into their adulthoods. When her husband, Samuel, was absent, at the request of parishioners Susanna would host gatherings in their kitchen to pray and read Scripture. While careful not to preach or defy restrictions on women's ecclesiastic roles, Susanna clearly demonstrated pastoral gifts as well as theological wisdom. She played a substantial role in shaping the Methodist movement through her influence on her sons John and Charles. And through their correspondence Susanna continued to inform John's theological contributions and leadership of the Methodist renewal movement.

6. Who are United Methodists today?

In 1968, The Evangelical United Brethren Church and The Methodist Church united to form a single denomination. Today The United Methodist Church has approximately twelve million members worldwide, with a vibrant presence in Europe, Asia, Africa, and the United States.

Theologically and historically, The United Methodist Church today represents the confluence of three streams of tradition: Methodism, the Church of the United Brethren in Christ, and The

Evangelical Association. It operates with a connectional structure that guides and supports ministry at local, regional, and global levels, and prioritizes an emphasis on God's grace, personal piety, and social action in its teaching and practice.

7. Where are United Methodists located in the world?

When The United Methodist Church was created in 1968, it had approximately eleven million members, making it one of the largest Protestant denominations in the world. Since then The United Methodist Church has become increasingly aware of itself as a world church with membership and conferences in Africa, Asia, Europe, and the United States.

United Methodist membership today numbers around twelve million members. Membership in Europe and the United States has decreased, while there has been growth in membership in parts of Africa and Asia, including Sierra Leone, Côte d'Ivoire, the Democratic Republic of Congo, Zimbabwe, Mozambique, South Africa, and the Philippines.

The General Conference, which meets every four years with delegates from across the world, reflects our global nature. Written reports and legislation for the conference are provided in English, French, Portuguese, and Swahili, while oral interpretation during the conference is offered in these languages as well as German, Russian, Spanish, Korean, American Sign Language, and others as needed for a given year.

(Adapted from *The Book of Discipline,* "A Brief History of The United Methodist Church," p. 23)

8. How is The United Methodist Church different from other Christian denominations?

Methodism began as a renewal movement, which is different from the way many other Christian denominations began (see question 9 for more on that). In terms of beliefs, United Methodism has a number of distinctive emphases that go back to our founder, John Wesley.

One such distinction is an emphasis on God's grace. Grace pervades our understanding of Christian faith and life. By grace we mean the undeserved, unmerited, and loving action of God in human existence through the ever-present Holy Spirit. John Wesley described grace in three ways: prevenient, justifying, and sanctifying grace.

Another distinctive emphasis is justification and assurance. In justification we are, through faith, forgiven our sin and restored to God's favor. This process of justification and new birth is often referred to as conversion. Such a change may be sudden and dramatic, or gradual and cumulative. It marks a new beginning, yet it is part of an ongoing process. Christian experience as personal transformation always expresses itself as faith working by love.

Our Wesleyan theology also embraces the scriptural promise that we can expect to receive assurance of our present salvation as the Spirit "bears witness with our spirit that we are children of God."

We also place particular emphasis on sanctification, or continual growth in grace. We hold that the wonder of God's acceptance and pardon does not end God's saving work. Through the power of the Holy Spirit, we are enabled to increase in the knowledge and love of God and in love for our neighbor. New birth is the first step in this process of sanctification, which leads toward what Wesley called Christian perfection, that is, a heart "habitually filled with the love of God and neighbor" and as "having the mind of Christ and walking as he walked."

United Methodists also believe that both faith and good works have a role in the Christian life. Faith is the only response essential for salvation. However, our salvation finds expression in good works. Both faith and good works belong within an all-encompassing theology of grace, since they stem from God's gracious love "shed abroad in our hearts by the Holy Spirit."

United Methodists also place a high priority on mission and service. We insist that personal salvation always involves Christian mission and service to the world. By joining heart and hand, we assert that personal religion, evangelical witness, and Christian social action are reciprocal and mutually reinforcing. We recognize that love of God is always linked with love of neighbor, a passion for justice, and renewal in the life of the world.

Finally, we emphasize the nurturing and serving function of Christian fellowship in the Church. The personal experience of faith is nourished by the worshipping community.

For Wesley there is no religion but social religion, no holiness but social holiness. The communal forms of faith in the Wesleyan tradition not only promote personal growth; they also equip and mobilize us for mission and service to the world.

(Adapted from The Book of Discipline, ¶102,
"Our Distinctive Heritage as United Methodists"
and "Distinctive Wesleyan Emphases," pp. 51–54)

9. What does The United Methodist Church have in common with other denominations?

United Methodists share a common heritage with Christians of every age and nation. This heritage is grounded in belief in Jesus Christ as Savior and Lord (*The Book of Discipline*, pp. 47–48).

With other Christians, we confess belief in the triune God—Father, Son, and Holy Spirit. This confession embraces the biblical witness to God's activity in creation, encompasses God's gracious self-involvement in the dramas of history, and anticipates the consummation of God's reign.

We hold in common with all Christians a faith in the mystery of salvation in and through Jesus Christ. At the heart of the gospel of salvation is God's Incarnation in Jesus of Nazareth. Scripture witnesses to the redeeming love of God in Jesus's life and teachings, his atoning death, his resurrection, his sovereign presence in history, his triumph over the powers of evil and death, and his promised return.

We share the Christian belief that God's redemptive love is realized in human life by the activity of the Holy Spirit, both in personal experience and in the community of believers, the church.

We understand ourselves to be part of Christ's universal church, and we are initiated and incorporated into this community of faith by baptism, receiving the promise of the Spirit that re-creates and transforms us. With other Christians we regularly have Holy Communion, where we participate in the risen presence of Jesus Christ and are thereby nourished for faithful discipleship. We pray and work for the coming of God's realm and reign to the world and rejoice in the promise of everlasting life that overcomes death and the forces of evil.

With other Christians we recognize that the reign of God is both a present and future reality. The church is called to be that place where the first signs of the reign of God are identified and acknowledged in the world. We also look to the end time in which God's work will be fulfilled. This prospect gives us hope in our present actions as individuals and as the church.

Finally, we share with many Christian communions a recognition of the authority of Scripture in matters of faith, the confession that our justification as sinners is by grace through faith, and the sober realization that the church is in need of continual reformation and renewal.

(Adapted from *The Book of Discipline,* ¶102,
"Our Common Heritage as Christians" and
"Basic Christian Affirmations," pp. 47, 49–50)

10. *Who are the leaders in The United Methodist Church?*

The United Methodist Church has leadership at every level of the Church, from the local church up through the global church.

Leadership includes ordained clergy: elders, deacons, and bishops. But an important feature of Methodism in general and The United Methodist Church in particular is the active involvement of lay leaders—that is, those who aren't ordained—at all levels of the Church.

While John Wesley and many influential leaders in the early Methodist movement were ordained in the Church of England, the movement grew in large part thanks to the widespread and involved leadership of laypersons. In the early Methodist renewal movement, Methodist laypeople had greater influence than preachers or clergy in facilitating conviction, sanctification, and other significant spiritual experiences. This is because the most frequent social context for early Methodist conversions was solitude, followed by small groups, where laypersons were most often the primary leaders. When Methodism took root in the United States, circuit-riding preachers would visit churches to preach and administer the sacraments periodically, maybe once a month. The rest of the time, laypeople would teach and provide spiritual care.

This tradition continues today with lay leadership in the local church. While the pastor is the person responsible for spiritual leadership of a congregation, much of the ministry—teaching Sunday school and other classes, mission and outreach, and acts of care and compassion for one another—is carried out by the church's members. The same is true for much practical leadership, which happens through lay-driven committees such as trustees, finance, and pastor-parish relations. At gatherings beyond the church—at annual and jurisdictional conferences and General

Conference—there are always an equal number of lay and clergy delegates. The same is true of the various boards and agencies that serve the whole Church.

While ordained clergy provide leadership throughout The United Methodist Church, laypersons are also actively involved as leaders across the denomination.

11. Does The United Methodist Church have priests or ministers like other churches? What about bishops or a pope?

Like most Christian denominations, The United Methodist Church has ordained clergy, who are set apart and ordained for leadership, teaching, and administration of the sacraments in churches. The UMC does not use the language of "priests"; rather we call our ordained ministry leaders pastors, preachers, or elders.

There are two kinds of clergy in The UMC: elders and deacons.

What is an Ordained Deacon? Deacons are clergy leaders who are called by God, authorized by the Church, and ordained by a bishop to a lifetime ministry of Word, Service, Compassion, and Justice (¶329). Deacons exemplify Christian discipleship by being a bridge between the Church and society.

What is an Ordained Elder? Elders are ordained to a lifetime ministry of service, word, sacrament, and order. They are authorized to preach and teach God's Word, to administer the sacraments of baptism and Holy Communion, and to order the life of the Church for mission and ministry. Elders typically serve as the pastor of a local church, though some are appointed to extension ministries beyond the Church in non-profits and para-church organizations.

The United Methodist Church also has a kind of leader called a licensed local pastor. These are leaders of a local church (often smaller congregations) who are not ordained, but rather are licensed to preach, teach, and administer sacraments within their local ministry context. While ordained elders have the authority to perform sacraments anywhere, local pastors have the authority to do so only within their church.

The United Methodist Church also has bishops. These are ordained elders who are elected to supervise the clergy members of an annual conference, or sometimes multiple conferences. One of their most important roles is to appoint pastors to each church in their annual conference and otherwise promote the vitality of the congregations and pastors in their charge. The United Methodist Church does not have a pope or a lead bishop; instead, we have a Council of Bishops made of all active and retired bishops in the denomination. The Council of Bishops does have an elected president and other officers who lead and speak for the council.

12. What is the role of ordained clergy in The United Methodist Church?

United Methodists consider ordination to ministry a gift from God to the church. In ordination, the church affirms and continues the ministry that began with the early church's apostles through persons empowered by the Holy Spirit today. Those who are ordained make a commitment to consciously live according to the gospel and to proclaim the gospel to the world.

Those who are ordained in The United Methodist Church are called to lead God's people through ministries of service, word, sacrament, order, compassion, and justice. The Church's ministry of service is a primary representation of God's love. Deacons respond to God's call to lead in Service, Word, Compassion, and Justice, and they equip others for this ministry through teaching, proclamation, and worship. Elders lead through preaching and teaching the Word of God, administration of the sacraments, ordering the Church for its mission and service, and administration of the discipline of the Church.

Ordained persons uphold a covenant with all Christians, especially with those whom they lead and serve in ministry. They also live by a covenant of care and accountability for one another—that is, with all those who are ordained in The United Methodist Church and especially with those who are in their same annual conference. For both deacons and elders, ministry is a lifetime commitment, and those who enter into it dedicate their whole lives to the personal and spiritual disciplines it requires.

(Adapted from *The Book of Discipline*, ¶303, p. 224)

13. What does it take to be ordained in The United Methodist Church?

To be ordained as an elder or as a deacon begins with a person's discernment of a call to ministry. According to *The Book of*

Discipline, "Those whom the Church ordains shall be conscious of God's call to ordained ministry, and their call shall be acknowledged and authenticated by the Church" (*The Book of Discipline*, ¶304). God's call can and does take many forms. In recognizing God's call in a person, the Church seeks evidence of faith and commitment to Jesus Christ, spiritual discipline, generosity, a recognition of God's call for themselves, commitment to leadership and service, evidence of God's gifts for ministry, and other qualities described in *The Book of Discipline*.

The process for ordination includes certification of a candidate for ministry and interviews with district and conference boards of ordained ministry as the person's candidacy continues. It also includes specific educational requirements depending on the kind of ordination sought, as well as written and oral examinations to verify a person's theological knowledge and understanding and ability to teach and lead.

Persons are ordained first to provisional membership in an annual conference and later to full membership. The ordination itself happens in a worship service, usually at an annual conference gathering. The process from first hearing God's call to full ordination usually takes many years.

14. Does The United Methodist Church ordain women?

Yes, The United Methodist Church ordains women as elders and as deacons, and welcomes the leadership and ministry of women at all levels of the Church.

John Wesley and Methodists also supported women's leadership in church settings. United Methodists continue to support the ordination of women, which was formally adopted by The Methodist Church's General Conference in 1956. Distinctive among Christian traditions, alongside Quakers and other smaller Christian communities, early Methodism maintained a space for women to preach and lead within the movement. In early British Methodism, women assumed numerous roles from preacher, leader of classes and bands, sick visitor, nurse, prayer leader, Sunday school teacher, and school operator. This support for women's roles and contributions carried into American Methodism. Indeed, Antoinette Brown Blackwell (1825–1921), the first woman to receive ordination in the United States, was ordained by a Wesleyan minister, Rev. Luther Lee, in 1853.

While there remains room for continued expansion of opportunities for women to share their gifts, each year women assume a greater number of leadership roles within Methodism as ordained ministers, district superintendents, general secretaries of agencies, and bishops. The United Methodist Church's General Commission on the Status and Role of Women advocates for full participation of women in the total life of The United Methodist Church. Their aim is to help the Methodists recognize every person—clergy and lay, women and men, adults and children—as full and equal parts of God's human family.

15. *How is the United Methodist denomination organized?*

United Methodism consists of a structure of conferences with interrelated accountability (charge, annual, district, jurisdictional/central, and General) and support that visibly represents connection and guides the ministry of the Church. The most authoritative body in The United Methodist Church is the General Conference. Next in the connectional organization are jurisdictional conferences (of which there are five in the United States) and numerous central conferences in regions around the world (which carry out delegated duties from the General Conference). Jurisdictional and central conferences mediate between the General Conference and annual conferences. In the United States, district conferences support the annual conference and missionary annual conferences, connecting it with local congregations, which are also organized into charge conferences.

16. *What are the general agencies of The United Methodist Church?*

In addition to conferences, a number of councils and agencies function within the structure of The United Methodist Church. These bodies function in distinctive and significant ways to connect and integrate ministries and resources across the denomination. These entities, at their best, provide leadership and contributions to the life of the denomination for the purpose of fulfilling our mission to participate in God's work in the world.

The general agencies may be organized into categories. For example, the Connectional Table and the General Council on Finance and Administration are supervisory councils. Following General Conference in 1972, the four basic program components were identified as General Board of Church and Society (Advocacy); General Board of Discipleship (Nurture); General Board of Global Ministries including the United Methodist Commission on Relief (Outreach); and General Board of Higher Education and Ministry (Vocation).

With these four program boards, three other general commissions are listed among them in the *Discipline*: the General Commission on Religion and Race, the General Commission on United Methodist Men, and the General Commission on the Status and Role of Women. Administrative units include the General Board of Pensions, The United Methodist Publishing House, General Commission on Archives and History, General Commission on Communication, Standing Committee on Central Conference Matters, and JUSTPEACE Center for Mediation and Conflict Transformation.

WHAT WE BELIEVE

17. What do United Methodists believe about salvation?

Often, when we hear salvation we think first of heaven—to be saved means that you go to heaven when you die. United Methodists believe that this tells only part of the story. While salvation from God in Jesus Christ through the Holy Spirit does include afterlife, resurrection of the body, and reuniting with the communion of saints, those dimensions only scratch the surface of a scriptural understanding of salvation.

When surveying Scripture to better understand the meaning of God's salvation in our lives, we find many more layers than simply an eternal rest in heaven. In every reference, salvation is God's work, God's work alone. According to biblical scholars, salvation in the Old and New Testaments is both individual and social—as well as cosmic, since Scripture tells us all creation will be redeemed. John Wesley and the early Methodists shared these scriptural themes relating to salvation.

John Wesley provides context for understanding salvation in the opening paragraph of his sermon "The Scripture Way of Salvation" written in 1765, which represents his most mature theology. John explicitly states salvation is not only "going to heaven or paradise." According to John, "The end is, in one word, salvation: the means to attain it, faith." He continues, "It is easily discerned, that these two little words, I mean faith and salvation, include the substance of all the Bible, the marrow, as it were, of the whole Scripture."

John Wesley describes salvation as available now. Living into the wholeness of God's salvation in Jesus Christ through the Holy Spirit for us through grace alone changes everything. When we receive God's grace, we experience salvation, not only the ultimate wholeness of union with the Triune God, but the assurance now of reconciled relationships with God and others. Through our baptism we are initiated into the body of Christ and commissioned to love God and neighbor in our words and lives. This new identity as children of God gives us purpose and peace in the midst of a troubled world as we participate in God's unfolding work.

18. What is grace? Why is it so important for United Methodists?

Grace is a central belief for United Methodists. By grace we mean the free gift of God's redeeming love in Jesus Christ through the Holy Spirit. United Methodists believe grace is therefore the foundation of what it means to be Christian. God's grace pervades all of creation and is universally present. According to United Methodist resources, grace is God's presence to create, heal, forgive, reconcile, and transform human hearts and creation.

John Wesley provides further guidance for understanding grace in his sermon "The Scripture Way of Salvation," in which he categorizes grace as prevenient, justifying, and sanctifying.

19. What is prevenient grace?

Prevenient grace means the grace that "comes before."

God's prevenient grace precedes our awareness, leading us toward God and one another for the purpose of receiving God's grace and salvation. Every person is created in the image and likeness of God, though we are all fallen. And God's grace, beginning with prevenient grace, is consistently working within each of us. Prevenient grace precedes, or comes before, one's awareness of God. It is the grace that pushes and pulls—consistently guiding persons created in the image of God to seek God's grace and salvation. One essential purpose of grace, initiated by prevenient grace, is to restore the image of God, God's goodness, in persons.

20. What is justifying grace?

Justifying grace, or justification, is the work of God in persons imputing Jesus Christ's righteousness by planting the seeds of salvation, pardoning or forgiving sin through faith. Justification is the gift of grace through faith alone and is the work of God in Christ through Jesus's atonement, life, death, and resurrection.

Justification is what God does for us in Christ. Justification results in a new relationship between God and the believer. Through justification we are freed from the guilt of sin and receive assurance of our salvation. Assurance is the witness of God's Holy Spirit with our spirit that we are children of God. This is not necessarily an assurance of heaven or final salvation, but an assurance of God's love for us as children of God.

In Sunday school sometimes we are taught that God's justifying grace makes me "just as if I never sinned." In response to justifying grace, one repents of sin and receives an assurance of one's salvation. For United Methodists drawing on Scripture and John Wesley, justification most often occurs as an event, not a process. At justification the process of sanctification begins.

21. What is sanctifying grace?

Sanctification is God's work through the Holy Spirit in us. John Wesley describes sanctification as "saved from sin, and perfected in love." Through sanctifying grace, God's image is renewed in us as we grow in holiness, evidenced in our expressions of love for God, neighbor, and creation. In sanctification Christ's righteousness is imparted to us. Sanctification is a real change in the life of believers. Sanctification is most often a process that begins in persons at the time of justification. In sanctification one lives into the changed relationship with God and is changed from within by God's Holy Spirit. Because of sanctifying grace we find ourselves participating in good works and growing into an ever-deepening faith, not to earn grace, but as its resulting fruit that nurtures further growth—or as Wesley described it, "perfected in love."

22. What are the means of grace?

Means of grace are an important aspect of our Wesleyan heritage. However, they are not merely a point of historical posterity of an archaic movement. Means of grace are a significant aspect of a vital living tradition. Means of grace are practices, recognized by Christian tradition, that help shape personal and communal faith. They are means by which personal and communal spiritual formation may be formed and cultivated.

John Wesley desired to embody holy living. He felt that the means of grace should be used constantly thus combining the inner with the outer expressions of salvation (and his doctrines of justification and sanctification).

John Wesley defined the means of grace as "the ordinary channels of conveying [God's] grace into the souls of [persons]." Wesley divided the means of grace into two groups: instituted and prudential. The instituted means of grace roughly corresponded to traditional Christian understandings of works of piety, or development of personal holiness. The prudential means of grace corresponded to traditional Christian understandings of works of mercy or expressions of social holiness. It is important to remember that within the Wesleyan tradition the means of grace, although described separately, are never meant to be understood or practiced separately.

The instituted means of grace include prayer, searching the Scriptures, the Lord's Supper, fasting, and Christian conferencing. Wesley understood these as works of piety. The prudential means of grace are designated works of mercy and described as relating to the bodies and souls of persons such as feeding the hungry, clothing the naked, entertaining the stranger, visiting those who are in prison, sick, or variously afflicted, instructing the seeker, awakening the sinner, quickening the lukewarm, confirming the wavering, comforting the afflicted, succoring the tempted, or contributing in any manner to the saving of souls.

23. Do United Methodists believe in salvation by faith alone?

Yes, United Methodists believe that we are saved by God alone.

Accepting and relying on God's grace for salvation is the most important component of Christian faith. Often, we neglect to attend to the most pressing truth about God's grace and salvation: There is nothing more, or anything less, one can do to earn God's love and eternal salvation. Nothing. One needs only to accept God's love and grace. Acceptance, that is all.

24. What is the relationship between faith and action in United Methodism?

John Wesley offers helpful perspective on the role of good works. Wesley struggled for much of his early life and ministry with the role and place of good works in salvation.

When Christian believers practice good works, we respond to God's love in gratitude by accepting the biblical invitation to love God and neighbor. Good works respond to God's gift of grace, and through those good works, God brings us to share in God's holiness and justice. As Wesley explained in his sermon "Justification by Faith," good works follow justification. We don't earn salvation or justification by good works, but good works are evidence of our changed heart and life that emerge naturally as we respond to God's grace and strive to follow Jesus wholeheartedly.

25. What sacraments does The United Methodist Church observe?

Methodists, with other Protestants, recognize two sacraments based on Jesus's ministry described in Scripture: baptism and the Lord's Supper. Through baptism individuals confess our belief in the Triune God, repent of our sins, accept God's grace in Jesus Christ through the Holy Spirit, and are initiated into the body of Christ. United Methodists practice infant baptism, though for those baptized as infants, confirmation when they are older (usually around sixth grade) is an opportunity for them to profess their faith for themselves and assume the responsibility of leading a Christian life.

In the Lord's Supper, also known as Holy Communion or the Eucharist, we remember God's gift of Jesus Christ through bread and wine (although in most UMC churches we use grape juice instead of wine). In Communion we experience God's gift of

Christ through the Holy Spirit as the community of faith, gathered to receive God's gift in the bread and juice, and then to be sent out as the body of Christ to the world.

26. Who can receive Holy Communion in The United Methodist Church?

Unlike some other denominations, United Methodists practice "open table" Communion, meaning that anyone with a sincere desire to receive Christ is welcome. You need not be a member of a United Methodist church, or any church, in order to receive Communion. Rather, as our Communion liturgy states, "Christ our Lord invites to his table all who love him, who earnestly repent of their sins, and seek to live in peace with one another" (*The United Methodist Hymnal*, "A Service of Word and Table I," p. 7).

United Methodists believe that Communion is a vessel of God's grace, and as such it can mediate God's grace and love to all.

27. What is confirmation, and why is it important?

Confirmation is the process by which we are confirmed as members of the church universal and as members of The United Methodist Church. To become a professing member of the Church, one must be baptized and profess the Christian faith, as well as take vows of membership. For those baptized as adults, confirmation happens at the same time as baptism. But for those baptized as infants or very young children, confirmation is an opportunity for them to profess faith for themselves. It typically happens after a period of instruction about the meaning of faith, central beliefs, and the history of the church, and the importance of the decision to profess faith.

Preparation for the experience of profession of faith and confirmation is provided regularly for adults and for youth in sixth grade and above.

Confirmation happens in a worship service. Using the services of the baptismal covenant, youth who were baptized as children will now profess their faith, commit themselves to a life of discipleship, and be confirmed. Confirmation is both a human act of commitment and the gracious action of the Holy Spirit strengthening and empowering discipleship. Youth and adults who have not been baptized who wish to profess faith and join The United Methodist Church are candidates for baptism and will be both baptized and confirmed during the service.

When persons unite as professing members with a local United Methodist church, they profess their faith in God, the Father Almighty, maker of heaven and earth; in Jesus Christ his only Son; and in the Holy Spirit. Thus, they make known their desire to live their daily lives as disciples of Jesus Christ. They covenant together with God and with the members of the local church to keep the vows that are a part of the order of confirmation and reception into the Church, including repentance of sin; acceptance of freedom and power to resist evil; trust in Jesus as Lord and Savior; and loyalty to the Church through prayers, presence, gifts, service, and witness.

(Adapted from *The Book of Discipline,* ¶217, p. 157)

28. What special books do United Methodists rely on?

The most important text for Christians, including United Methodists, is the Bible. For United Methodists, Scripture is inspired by God and authoritative in the lives of Christian believers. From Scripture we receive all we need to experience God's invitation to salvation in Jesus Christ through the Holy Spirit. Methodist doctrine or beliefs are grounded in Scripture. Scripture shapes our understanding of God's grace for all. It teaches us how to grow in God's grace and holiness as well as how to share God's grace with others.

Other important texts include *The United Methodist Hymnal* and *The United Methodist Book of Worship*. The pattern of worship United Methodists share, often described as "Word and Table," can be found in the first few pages of our hymnal. *The Book of Worship* contains services to guide other worship, such as funerals and weddings. *The Book of Worship* and the *Hymnal* provide guides and resources to facilitate worship in local churches, conferences, and beyond. They contribute to our connectionalism by providing shared experiences. Both the *Book of Worship* and the *Hymnal* are grounded in Scripture and demonstrate Wesleyan doctrinal emphases, especially themes of grace.

The United Methodist Hymnal is also important because it contains our hymns. From the earliest days of the renewal movement led by the Wesleys, Methodists have been known as "a singing people." Next to Scripture, Methodist hymnals continue to be one of the most formative resources in the lives of individuals and communities of faith.

The primary purpose of hymn-singing in the early Methodist renewal movement was Christian formation in Scripture and doctrine. Charles's poetry sung widely as hymns more than anything else formed the early Methodists. Charles Wesley's poems set to music, often well-loved tunes, contributed significantly to the energy and doctrine of the early Methodist movement, which continues today. Some claim as much as 85 percent of the Bible may be present in the hymns composed by Charles Wesley.

The Book of Discipline is also a key text for United Methodists, as it contains the organizational principles and theological underpinnings for our shared way of life. The General Conference, which meets every four years, is responsible for revising and updating our *Book of Discipline*. *The Book of Resolutions of The United Methodist Church*, also revised and updated by the General Conference, contains official statements of The United Methodist Church on a range of pressing issues in the world today.

These are the most important texts for United Methodists. At the same time, while John Wesley never shifted from the prioritization of Scripture in the lives of believers, he did not only read Scripture. To grow in relationship with God, neighbor, and creation, Wesley read widely and deeply—alongside Scripture as well as numerous translations and versions of Scripture. John Wesley argued vehemently against Christians ONLY reading the Bible. Instead, he encouraged Christians to seek other sources and resources to read alongside Scripture to deepen and strengthen a relationship with God and facilitate sanctifying grace, God's holiness, in believers.

29. What do United Methodists believe about the Bible? How do they read and interpret the Bible?

United Methodists believe the Holy Bible, both the Old and New Testaments, reveals the Word of God so far as it is necessary for our salvation. We receive it through the Holy Spirit as the true rule and guide for faith and practice.

United Methodists share with other Christians the conviction that Scripture is the primary source and criterion for Christian doctrine. At the same time, we are convinced that Jesus Christ—not the Bible—is the living Word of God in our midst. The Bible points us to Christ, whom we trust in life and death. The biblical authors, illumined by the Holy Spirit, bear witness that in Christ the world is reconciled to God.

United Methodists believe that as we open our minds and hearts to the Word of God through the words of human beings inspired by the Holy Spirit, faith is born and nourished, our understanding is deepened, and the possibilities for transforming the world become apparent to us.

While we acknowledge the primacy of Scripture in theological reflection, our attempts to grasp its meaning always involve tradition, experience, and reason. We properly read Scripture within the believing community, informed by the tradition of that community.

We interpret individual texts in light of their place in the Bible as a whole. We are aided by scholarly inquiry and personal insight, under the guidance of the Holy Spirit. As we work with each text, we take into account what we have been able to learn about the original context and intention of that text. In this understanding we draw upon the careful historical, literary, and textual studies of recent years, which have enriched our understanding of the Bible.

Through this faithful reading of Scripture, we may come to know the truth of the biblical message in its bearing on our own lives and the life of the world. Thus, the Bible serves both as a source of our faith and as the basic criterion by which the truth and fidelity of any interpretation of faith is measured.

Like Scripture, these may become creative vehicles of the Holy Spirit as they function within the Church. They quicken our faith, open our eyes to the wonder of God's love, and clarify our understanding.

(Adapted from *The Book of Discipline,* ¶104, p. 73,
and ¶105, "Our Theological Task," pp. 80–91)

30. What do United Methodists believe about Jesus Christ?

United Methodists hold in common with all Christians a faith in the mystery of salvation in and through Jesus Christ. At the heart of the gospel of salvation is God's Incarnation in Jesus of Nazareth. Scripture witnesses to the redeeming love of God in Jesus's life and teachings, his atoning death, his resurrection, his sovereign presence in history, his triumph over the powers of evil and death, and his promised return. Because God truly loves us in spite of our willful sin, God judges us, summons us to repentance, pardons us, receives us by that grace given to us in Jesus Christ, and gives us hope of life eternal.

The historic creeds of the church, particularly the Apostles' Creed and the Nicene Creed, express our belief about Jesus Christ, which we share with all Christians. We profess faith in Jesus Christ as fully God and fully human, in whom the divine and human natures are perfectly and inseparably united. We believe that he is the eternal Word made flesh, the only begotten Son of the Father, born of the Virgin Mary by the power of the Holy Spirit. As ministering Servant he lived, suffered, and died on the cross. He was buried, rose from the dead, and ascended into heaven to be with the Father, from whence he shall return. He is eternal Savior and Mediator, who intercedes for us, and by him all men will be judged.

(Adapted from *The Book of Discipline,* ¶102 and ¶104, pp. 49 and 73)

31. *What does The United Methodist Church believe and teach about current issues in the world?*

The United Methodist Church has a long history of concern for social justice. Its members have often taken forthright positions on controversial issues involving Christian principles. Early Methodists expressed their opposition to the slave trade, to smuggling, and to the cruel treatment of prisoners.

Today, the Social Principles in our *Book of Discipline* guide us in responding to the pressing issues of our world. The Social Principles, while not to be considered Church law, are a prayerful and thoughtful effort on the part of the General Conference to speak to the human issues in the contemporary world from a sound biblical and theological foundation as historically demonstrated in United Methodist traditions. They are a call to faithfulness and are intended to be instructive and persuasive in the best of the prophetic spirit. The Social Principles are a call to all members of The United Methodist Church to a prayerful, studied dialogue of faith and practice.

(Adapted from *The Book of Discipline*,
"Preface to the Social Principles," pp. 105–6)

The Book of Resolutions contains all of the current and official social policies and other resolutions adopted by the General Conference of The United Methodist Church. These resolutions serve as official policy statements guiding the work and ministry of The United Methodist Church, as well as educational resources on important issues affecting the lives of people and God's creation.

(Adapted from *The Book of Resolutions*, p. 21)

Together, the Social Principles and *The Book of Resolutions* guide us in relating faith to life and action, helping us to respond to injustice and other pressing needs we see around us.

32. Who decides what The United Methodist Church believes and teaches?

Within United Methodism, the General Conference is the authoritative body and voice. It is the only entity with authority to speak for the denomination. This includes theological and doctrinal statements. Typically, the General Conference meets every four years, or quadrennium, and consists of elected delegates from each annual conference across the denomination.

The General Conference has the authority to make changes to The United Methodist Church's *Book of Discipline*, including theological as well as practical matters, so long as those changes are in accordance with our constitution. (The constitution may be amended by a two-thirds majority at General Conference, followed by ratification by all the annual conferences.)

The Judicial Council (the United Methodist equivalent of a Supreme Court) interprets the constitution and has the ultimate authority to determine if a given change is constitutional or not. And the denomination's bishops are responsible for assuring that our clergy and churches follow *The Book of Discipline*.

Within each church, the pastor has authority to teach the congregation, which includes classes and preaching, as well as other forms of instruction.

WHAT WE DO

33. What do United Methodists do to practice their faith?

United Methodists believe that God calls us to love of God and neighbor. John Wesley characterized a Methodist as one who "has the love of God shed abroad in [one's] heart." United Methodism is about a living, practical faith.

United Methodists practice faith in many of the same ways as Christians of other denominations, including worship, prayer, reading and studying the Bible, meeting in small groups, and engaging in works of service and outreach.

United Methodists typically worship on Sundays, though some congregations may also hold services on Saturdays or other times throughout the week. Singing is a vital and valued part of United Methodist worship alongside the sermon, Scripture reading, offering, and affirmation of faith.

We also pray regularly and read the Bible. While these practices vary from one person to the next, we value daily prayer and regular Scripture reading as ways to grow in faith.

Just as important as reading the Bible alone is reading it and studying it alongside others. The use of small groups has been from the very first a key part of growth in grace for Methodists, and United Methodists today continue the practice with weekly small groups, home groups, and Sunday school classes for adults, children, and youth. We believe that when we gather for study and fellowship, we receive God's grace by learning from one another, bearing one another's burdens, and sharing God's love with one another.

John Wesley believed that worship, prayer, and Scripture study are works of piety and means of grace. But he also believed and taught that works of mercy—that is, caring for others, serving the poor and those in need, and advocating for the improvement of social conditions—are also means of grace. We receive God's grace when we practice works of love and charity. So serving others and advocating on their behalf are also important ways United Methodists practice our faith.

34. What are some distinctive United Methodist practices?

While many of the ways United Methodists practice our faith is held in common with those of other Christian denominations— for example worship, prayer, and Scripture study—The United Methodist Church and other Wesleyan denominations also have a number of distinctive practices.

One such practice is the use of small groups to grow in our faith. While many denominations gather in small groups for Bible study and fellowship, small groups have been part of Methodist

DNA from the very beginning. John Wesley found that gathering people into bands and classes allowed them to support one another in faith and share insights. Today this practice continues through a strong emphasis on Sunday school, small groups, and home groups, with the expectation that these groups will enable participants to grow in grace together.

Itinerant ministry is another distinctive United Methodist practice. Early Methodist preachers served multiple churches, traveling from one to another in a circuit where they would serve Communion and preach once a month (or more or less often) and teach before moving on to another church. Today this practice continues as United Methodist elders agree to moving by appointment within their annual conference, at their bishop's discretion.

The United Methodist Church has a long tradition of outreach and social justice, with a legacy of compassion and care evidenced through founding colleges, universities, and hospitals; advocating for the rights of women and minorities; and opposing slavery during the eighteenth and nineteenth centuries.

While none of these practices are unique to United Methodists, they are all emphasized in a distinct way in The United Methodist Church.

35. What is the role of the faith community, or the congregation, in The United Methodist Church?

The United Methodist Church places high value on the role of the local faith community, or local congregation, as the most significant place where we live as disciples of Jesus Christ. We regard the local church as a community of believers under the Lordship of Christ, where we hear God's Word read and proclaimed and receive the sacraments of baptism and Holy Communion.

Our *Book of Discipline* regards the local church as "a strategic base from which Christians move out to the structures of society . . . to help people to accept and confess Jesus Christ as Lord and Savior and to live their daily lives in light of their relationship with God" (*The Book of Discipline,* ¶201, p. 147). In the faith community we receive the guidance of the Holy Spirit and reach out in ministry and partnership with our broader community and participate in God's mission to restore the world.

36. What happens in a United Methodist worship service?

When we gather in local churches, most often on Sunday mornings but also throughout the week, we gather to worship the Triune God. All are welcome to share in this worshipful work, since it is at God's invitation that we gather in relationship with God, neighbor, and with all creation. Christian, and Methodist, worship is grounded in Scripture. Through the Holy Spirit and teachings of Scripture, patterns of worship connect to generations of believers. Our Christian worship continues to imitate practices led by Jesus Christ among his disciples and those he encountered.

Some aspects of our worship echo the practices of God's covenant people described in the Old Testament. Methodist worship shares patterns with the worldwide body of Christians, while also offering distinctives resulting in a recognizable ethos across United Methodism. And yet, while we share so much in common with Christian siblings across time and space, worship among United Methodists across the world also demonstrates the uniqueness of every local church gathering and even every worship service. Through the Holy Spirit we are unified in grace and truth, and in the Holy Spirit we are granted unique gifts and experiences.

The pattern of worship United Methodists share, often described as "Word and Table," can be found in the first few pages of our hymnal. We gather, often with music, to celebrate and proclaim our faith; we hear God's Word read and interpreted; and we respond to God's Word by affirming our faith, offering our gifts, and receiving Holy Communion. Finally we are sent forth from worship into the world with the understanding that we are to bear God's light and love to all.

Our United Methodist *Book of Worship* and the *Hymnal* provide guides and resources to facilitate worship in local churches, conferences, and beyond. They contribute to our connectionalism by providing shared experiences. Both the *Book of Worship* and the *Hymnal* are grounded in Scripture and demonstrate Wesleyan doctrinal emphases, especially themes of grace.

37. What kinds of music do you find in a United Methodist service?

Methodists have always held song as an essential part of our worship—we even teach and learn our beliefs more often through song than from texts. Singing hymns in communal worship is a moving and formational practice. Singing prayers and hymns with children teaches them and adults alike the simple and beautiful truths of God's love for us and all creation. In the later stages of dementia and Alzheimer's disease, persons demonstrating little to no awareness of their surroundings can seem miraculously present through singing familiar songs from deep in their memories. According to St. Augustine, to sing is to pray twice. Singing together in community has also been shown to encourage healing, particularly following lockdowns during the COVID-19 global pandemic.

From the earliest days of the renewal movement led by the Wesleys, Methodists have been known as "a singing people." Next to Scripture, Methodist hymnals continue to be one of the most formative resources in the lives of individuals and communities of faith. The current hymnal, published in 1989, provides a range of resources for community worship from hymns and psalms, prayers, and orders of service. The current hymnal provides worship resources from a wide diversity of creators with some stretching over one thousand years of use.

The primary purpose of hymn-singing in the early Methodist renewal movement was Christian formation in Scripture and doctrine. Charles's poetry sung widely as hymns more than anything else formed the early Methodists. John Wesley compiled the first hymnbook used in North America in 1737 for use during his ministry in Georgia. In his hymns, both instruments and products of the movement, Charles drew heavily from Scripture both in verbal allusions and imagery. In the hymnbook of 1780, John's arrangement of hymns was based on a pattern of spiritual experience, which could help guide formation in contexts that had less familiarity with Christian Scripture.

Charles Wesley's poems set to music, often well-loved tunes, contributed significantly to the energy and doctrine of the early Methodist movement, which continues today. *The United Methodist Hymnal* includes numerous hymns by Charles Wesley, each grounded in Scripture and formational for Christians growing in faith. Some claim as much as 85 percent of the Bible may be present in the hymns composed by Charles Wesley. The *Hymnal* is organized around Wesleyan emphases of doctrine, including grace—prevenient, justifying, and sanctifying.

38. How do United Methodists grow in faith?

John Wesley taught that growth in faith happens through participation in the means of grace—that is, the ordinary channels by which we experience God's grace through the Holy Spirit. These include both works of piety, such as prayer, Bible study, and Holy Communion, as well as works of mercy, such as serving those in need. (For more on the means of grace, see question 22.)

Wesley also taught about the importance of community as a vehicle for the Holy Spirit to empower us and enrich our faith. Wesley is well known for saying of Christianity, "Solitary religion is not to be found there. 'Holy solitaries' is a phrase no more consistent with the gospel than holy adulterers. The gospel of Christ knows of no religion but social; no holiness but social holiness" (preface to *Hymns and Sacred Poems*, 1739).

While extraordinary stories exist of individuals coming to and being sustained in Christian faith as solitary beings, this is very rare. As Wesley and the early Methodists realized, Christian faith—love of God and love of neighbor—is most fruitfully practiced in relationships within communities of faith. Through nurturing accountable relationships Methodism grew deeply in persons and expanded broadly through communities to share God's love in Jesus Christ through the Holy Spirit. This continues today in United Methodist support and emphasis on small groups as important vehicles for growing in faith.

39. What are the three general rules, or three simple rules, in United Methodism?

In 1743, as the Methodist small groups continued to grow and a network among them expanded throughout England, John Wesley wrote a series of simple "rules" to give these groups a common form and way of life to share in together, which we today regard as the three General Rules: (1) doing no harm and avoiding evil of every kind; (2) doing good, and (3) attending upon the ordinances of God. Thanks to a popular book titled *Three Simple Rules* by Rueben Job, United Methodists today sometimes remember these general rules as, "Do no harm. Do good. Stay in love with God."

To this day, these General Rules stand like guideposts marking the course of Methodist life—they are part of our distinct understanding of doctrine. The General Rules and their description as means of grace show Christians within The United Methodist Church the way to practice their faith against the backdrop of our deep, historically shared doctrinal commitments. Individuals in covenant with their brothers and sisters in Christ nurture their faith in the Triune God together through common devotional practices like prayer and sharing in the Lord's Supper, while also serving their neighbors through practices of mercy. The first two rules relate, again, to the orientation of Christian life: they are about actions, what we do together, and how those actions are tangible, embodied expressions of mercy, grace, and love.

The General Rules' third component, the "ordinances of God," consisted of what Wesley often referred to as the means of grace. In the context of their bands and classes, Christians would encourage one another in their Christian journeys by asking: How are you praying? Where are you serving others, visiting the sick and those who are imprisoned? By holding each other accountable to these practices, these believers helped one another come to know faith in the Triune God. Some of these means of grace emphasized individual spiritual growth through public and private prayer, Scripture study, confession, fasting, and participating in worship. Other practices were more about how you shared in God's mercy and love at work in the world, like feeding your hungry neighbors, clothing those without adequate shelter, and visiting the imprisoned, sick, and afflicted. Interestingly, at times Wesley prioritized these works of mercy over individual devotional activities. He emphasized Methodists participating in acts of service as a way of correcting a tendency he saw too often in the church in his day, where Anglican teaching and practice focused on personal devotion to the minimization or even exclusion of Christian service.

40. What is the role of small groups or Bible studies in The United Methodist Church?

At its heart, the "method" of Methodism is a way of bringing us together to know God more deeply by practicing our faith alongside others. From our earliest days, small groups continue to be our best vehicle for people accepting God's grace in Jesus Christ and continuing their growth through the Holy Spirit. By practicing the means of grace in small groups and in daily individual life, we sustain and deepen Christian faith. Along with preaching and missional outreach, small groups for discipleship are a critical component of the Methodist ecology for receiving and sharing God's grace.

Small groups have been and continue to be one of the most vital spaces for Christian formation with God and one another. There is an opportunity to study, reflect, challenge, and discover. In small group settings we can experience vulnerability and accountability in the midst of encouragement and hospitality. Seemingly endless research demonstrates the effectiveness of small group spaces for learning, character formation, community building, and recovery from trauma as well as addictions. Small groups are most often sites of God's gift of salvation.

41. I hear a lot about conferences and conferencing in The United Methodist Church. What's that about?

In the Wesleyan tradition, conferencing remains a means of grace since it is a significant gathering for our experience in Christian community as United Methodists. Beginning with John Wesley's leadership, gathering for worship, fellowship, and planning the work of ministry was a means to receive and to share God's grace. As the early Methodist movement spread across the British Isles and increased in numbers, Wesley gathered the preachers in conference. These gatherings demonstrated and embodied the interrelated spiritual and operational dynamics of the connection that facilitated the ministry of the early Methodist movement. In our strongest and most faithful moments, United Methodists gather to practice conferencing and embody our connectionalism.

Most, if not all, of the Methodist and Wesleyan traditions across the world continue to practice forms of conferencing. In The United Methodist Church, conferencing is embodied in both time and place—in bodies that meet at regular intervals from specific regions. This happens at multiple levels, ranging from the global (General Conference) to the regional (jurisdictional and central conferences, as well as annual conferences) to the local (charge conferences). Support and accountability at all of these levels represent our connection and guide the ministry of the Church.

Conferences remain the most significant connectional structures and gatherings within United Methodism. Conferences provide a thoughtful and agile structure for an international connection. As United Methodism continues to shift, this structure may experience even more opportunity to reflect the growing vitality of its witness and mission in international contexts.

42. What is a charge conference?

In the Methodist tradition, the local church is also known as a charge. So, a charge conference is the conference that takes place within the local church, typically once per year. The function and purpose of the local church are structured to facilitate participation in the broader Church's mission, both locally as well as through the connectional structure. The local church connects to the annual conference through a charge conference. The charge conference membership includes all members of the church council or other governing body of the church, as well as any retired ministers who are members of the church.

At a charge conference the district superintendent or another representative of the annual conference presides to worship, appoint leadership, make important decisions, and celebrate ministry in connection. Conferences in their various forms continue to facilitate the broader Church's mission to make disciples for the transformation of the world. This starts at the local church level with the charge conference.

43. What is an annual conference?

The annual conference, both currently and historically, is the basic organizational unit of the denomination. The annual conference connects local churches with the broader governing structure to facilitate participation in the mission of the Church. Annual conferences are also organized into districts to facilitate ministry and fellowship, though districts are not granted significant authority within the structure. While baptized persons hold membership in local churches, persons receiving ordination in The United Methodist Church hold membership in the annual conference. Annual conferences meet once a year. Similar to General, jurisdictional, and central conferences, delegates to these annual conferences consist of an equal number of clergy and laity. Since early Methodism and John Wesley's leadership, annual conferences are an opportunity to gather in worship, fellowship, and planning for ministry. Many describe annual conferences as family reunions.

44. What is a jurisdictional conference?

Jurisdictional conferences, like the General Conference, usually meet every four years within a month or two following General Conference. Jurisdictions meet in their regions, but simultaneously with other jurisdictional conferences. The jurisdictional conference, like the General Conference, also consists of delegates elected from annual conferences. Jurisdictional and central conferences have two main responsibilities: electing episcopal leaders and setting conference boundaries. Central conferences are very similar to jurisdictional conferences but exist outside the United States. In preparation for General Conference 2024, legislation was submitted to revise this structure for the purpose of practicing greater parity and recovering from the systemic sins of colonialism.

45. What is the General Conference?

Within United Methodism, the General Conference is the authoritative body and voice. It is the only entity with authority to speak for the denomination. Typically, the General Conference meets every four years, or quadrennium, and consists of elected delegates from each annual conference across the denomination. Bishops preside at General Conference sessions, having voice but no vote. The General Conference met for a regular session in 2016 and 2024 (the one in 2020 was effectively canceled due to the COVID-19 pandemic). Barring unforeseen circumstances, it will meet again in regular session in 2028 and 2032.

The General Conference is a legislative body consisting of more than a dozen committees that bring legislation to the plenary for consideration. Approved legislation appears in *The Book of Discipline*, which is published following each regular session of General Conference. Any United Methodist may submit a petition to General Conference for consideration. The General Conference also considers resolutions for inclusion in *The Book of Resolutions* also published following each General Conference regular session.

The General Conference usually meets quadrennially in late spring followed by the jurisdictional conferences in July.

46. What kinds of things do United Methodists do to serve others? Why is this important?

United Methodism continues a long and tenacious heritage of missional impact. The United Methodist Church's Commission on Relief, alongside the American Red Cross and other secular relief organizations, is well known for being one of the first agencies in and among the last to leave areas suffering from catastrophic natural or human-imposed violent disasters. We can speculate about why this is the case—perhaps effective leadership, planning, or strategic use of resources. While these may all be pertinent reasons for UMCOR's remarkable reputation, this distinctive missional impact grows from our Methodist roots.

From its beginnings, the early Methodist movement sought to inspire a renewed imagination for God's transformation in communities. While such transformation often refers to God's grace within individuals through holiness or sanctification, the earliest Methodists did not stop with the inner spiritual life. As Charles and John Wesley gathered with classmates and colleagues in Oxford, they contemplated the impact of the inner spiritual life on their Christian practices and love of neighbor. In contrast to other Christian traditions, Methodism did not begin with a set of beliefs to be defended. Methodism's missional character was innate from the very beginning. The beliefs grew and developed as layers in response to relationships nurtured in small groups and communities as discussed in previous chapters. Through interactions with others and the steady authentic building of relationships, Methodism's missional character continues to grow.

47. What kinds of outreach programs does The United Methodist Church support?

Methodism has a rich legacy of missional impact, beginning with works of charity and empowerment in and beyond small groups in early Methodism. John Wesley and early Methodists created initiatives for accessibility to microfinance, health care, and education. Building on a strong economic ethic from John Wesley and the early Methodists, Methodists in the United States established numerous hospitals and institutions of higher education. Methodists resisted the enslavement of African Americans, including all in their small groups and ministry. Methodists also affirmed the gifts of women, ordaining the first woman in the United States. While there is always more to learn and ways to grow in God's sanctification, Methodists continue to demonstrate significant advocacy for social justice—in these ways and others.

48. How do United Methodists promote justice and advocate for the needs of others?

John Wesley and early Methodists practiced racial equality in the midst of violent and insidious racial injustice. Wesley encouraged the Christian faith and ministry of numerous persons of African descent. The last letter John Wesley wrote before his death was to William Wilberforce, a well-known British politician and advocate for abolition. The letter communicated words of encouragement to Wilberforce and emphasized the importance of his cause to abolish slavery.

Early Methodist views on the enslavement of persons in the United States were characterized by Wesley's strong antislavery position, which Francis Asbury and Thomas Coke echoed. Early Methodist conference actions provided a blanket denunciation of slavery. Owners of enslaved persons were not permitted to participate or lead Methodist small groups or to serve in pastoral leadership. Sadly, over time these clear expectations shifted, creating exceptions, particularly in the South, leading up to the Civil War.

Methodists continue a legacy of working toward racial equality through mission impact as well as inclusion in Methodist communities and political advocacy. From Methodism's beginnings, Methodists in the United States advocated for equality by confronting owners of enslaved persons, welcoming persons of African American descent in small groups and congregations, as well as petitioning Congress for more just legal actions.

Today The United Methodist Church facilitates the voices of numerous caucus groups advocating for underrepresented persons on the basis of race and gender including African American, Asian American, Latinx/Hispanic, and Native American. In 2000, the

General Conference adopted the "Act of Repentance for Racism," which facilitates practices of lament and repentance for the Church's participation in racism and inequality across generations. While Methodists continue to practice love of God and neighbor in remarkable ways, as human beings we all have more to learn and need for growth as we participate in God's sanctification of us and the world.

In response to social challenges, Methodists formed the Methodist Federation for Social Service (MFSS) in Washington, DC, on December 3–4, 1907. Through this group and its leaders, Methodists participated in and eventually led within a Social Gospel movement, which was addressing social crises active in the early twentieth century. Through the Methodists' leadership in the Social Gospel movement, the Social Creed was developed and adopted by the Methodist Federal Council of Churches.

The Social Creed served as a symbol of both ecumenical and social commitment for the Methodist Federal Council of Churches. As the affirmations were adopted by member denominations, additional changes were often made, threatening the common text. In response the council undertook a series of revisions before 1912 that acknowledged the growing interest in social and economic issues. Two additional declarations were included, and the document was expanded to mention the family, child development, health, liquor traffic, and property.

The sixteen-point Social Creed adopted in 1912 served as the basic pronouncement of the Methodist Federal Council of Churches for twenty years, although there were tensions among the member denominations, leading to revisions and additions. Additional paragraphs were appended on topics such as community service, industrial conditions, and labor rights. In the years following 1912, a controversy emerged with regard to the language of the creed. Some construed the language as reserved for the ecumenical creeds of Christendom and favored instead the language of social ideals.

The Board of Christian Social Concerns was later formed in 1952 by an amalgamation of various groups to implement the denomination's social creed, reduce duplication of work, and provide a strategic and symbolic presence in Washington, DC, across from the Capitol. Methodists' important work of advocacy for social justice continues based in the same location through the General Board of Church and Society. United Methodists are the only church in the United States with a physical presence on Capitol Hill. The General Board of Church and Society also maintains a presence at the Church Center for the United Nations in New York City. The General Board of Church and Society provides a persistent voice and strategically works for social justice through advocacy of government policies and allocation of resources. The General Board cares for the Social Principles included in *The Book of Discipline* and *The Book of Resolutions*.

49. How do I become a United Methodist?

Becoming a United Methodist means becoming part of a United Methodist congregation. For adults who have previously been baptized, this means professing faith and taking the membership vows for joining a United Methodist church. According to *The Book of Discipline,*

> When persons unite as professing members with a local United Methodist church, they profess their faith in God, the Father Almighty, maker of heaven and earth; in Jesus Christ his only Son, and in the Holy Spirit. Thus, they make known their desire to live their daily lives as disciples of Jesus Christ. They covenant together with God and with the members of the local church to keep the vows which are a part of the order of confirmation and reception into the Church:

1. To renounce the spiritual forces of wickedness, reject the evil powers of the world, and repent of their sin;
2. To accept the freedom and power God gives them to resist evil, injustice, and oppression;
3. To confess Jesus Christ as Savior, put their whole trust in his grace, and promise to serve him as their Lord;
4. To remain faithful members of Christ's holy church and serve as Christ's representatives in the world;
5. To be loyal to Christ through The United Methodist Church and do all in their power to strengthen its ministries;
6. To faithfully participate in its ministries by their prayers, their presence, their gifts, their service, and their witness;

7. To receive and profess the Christian faith as contained in the Scriptures of the Old and New Testaments.

(*The Book of Discipline,* ¶217, p.157)

During the worship service, the person joining the congregation takes the following vows, with the pastor asking the questions and the new member responding, "I will":

As members of Christ's universal church,
will you be loyal to The United Methodist Church,
and do all in your power to strengthen its ministries?
I will.

As members of this congregation,
will you faithfully participate in its ministries
by your prayers, your presence,
your gifts, and your service?
I will.

(*The United Methodist Hymnal,* p. 38)

The first step is to find a local United Methodist congregation in your area and visit the church. Most churches will have an online presence, such as a website or Facebook page, where you can find out worship times and what to expect. Speak with a few members and get to know the people. Then talk to the pastor about your desire to join. They will tell you more about what it means to be a disciple of Jesus Christ in the United Methodist tradition and what it will mean to become a member of their United Methodist congregation.

50. Where can I learn more about The United Methodist Church?

The United Methodist Church's official website is www.umc .org. You can read there about who we are, basic beliefs, ways we serve in the world, news from throughout the Church, and more.

If you are interested in reading more about United Methodist beliefs, practices, and history, or about the life and teachings of John Wesley, you might find the following resources to be helpful:

American Methodism, Revised and Updated, by Ashley Boggan D., Russell E. Richey, Kenneth E. Rowe, and Jean Miller Schmidt

Unrelenting Grace: A United Methodist Way of Life, by Kenneth H. Carter Jr.

The Sermons of John Wesley: A Collection for the Christian Journey, ed. Kenneth J. Collins and Jason E. Vickers

Revival: Faith as Wesley Lived It, by Adam Hamilton

Five Marks of a Methodist: The Fruit of a Living Faith, by Steve Harper

Five Means of Grace: Experience God's Love the Wesleyan Way, by Elaine A. Heath

WHO WE ARE AND WHAT WE BELIEVE

Three Simple Rules: A Wesleyan Way of Living, by Rueben P. Job

Being United Methodist Christians: Living a Life of Grace and Hope, by Andy Langford, Ann Langford Duncan, and Sally Langford

The Methodist Book of Daily Prayer, by Matt Miofsky

Knowing Who We Are: The Wesleyan Way of Grace, by Laceye C. Warner

The Method of Our Mission: United Methodist Polity and Organization, by Laceye C. Warner

The Means of Grace Bible

The Wesley Study Bible

The Wesley Center Online at Northwest Nazarene University: http://wesley.nnu.edu/john-wesley

A SAMPLING OF KEY WESLEYAN TEXTS

Covenant Prayer

From John Wesley's Covenant Service, 1780

We are no longer our own, but thine.
Put us to what thou wilt, rank us with whom thou wilt.
Put us to doing, put us to suffering.
Let us be employed by thee or laid aside for thee,
exalted for thee or brought low for thee.
Let us be full, let us be empty.
Let us have all things, let us have nothing.
We freely and heartily yield all things
to thy pleasure and disposal.
And now, O glorious and blessed God,
Father, Son, and Holy Spirit,

thou art ours, and we are thine. So be it.

And the covenant which we have made on earth,

let it be ratified in heaven. Amen.

A United Methodist Communion Liturgy

From A Service of Word and Table I (*The United Methodist Hymnal*, pp. 6–11).

See also https://www.umcdiscipleship.org/book-of-worship /a-service-of-word-and-table-i-and-introductions-to-the-other -forms.

Bold text indicates the congregation's response.

THE GREAT THANKSGIVING*

The Lord be with you.

And also with you.

Lift up your hearts.

We lift them up to the Lord.

Let us give thanks to the Lord our God.

It is right to give our thanks and praise.

It is right, and a good and joyful thing,

always and everywhere to give thanks to you,

Father Almighty, creator of heaven and earth.

You formed us in your image

and breathed into us the breath of life.

When we turned away, and our love failed,
> your love remained steadfast.
You delivered us from captivity,
> made covenant to be our sovereign God,
> and spoke to us through the prophets.
And so,
> with your people on earth
> and all the company of heaven
> we praise your name and join their unending hymn:

Holy, holy, holy Lord, God of power and might,
heaven and earth are full of your glory.
> **Hosanna in the highest.**
Blessed is he who comes in the name of the Lord.
> **Hosanna in the highest.**

Holy are you, and blessed is your Son Jesus Christ.
Your Spirit anointed him
> to preach good news to the poor,
> to proclaim release to the captives
> > and recovering of sight to the blind,
> to set at liberty those who are oppressed,
> and to announce that the time had come
> > when you would save your people.
He healed the sick, fed the hungry, and ate with sinners.
By the baptism of his suffering, death, and resurrection

you gave birth to your church,
delivered us from slavery to sin and death,
and made with us a new covenant
by water and the Spirit.
When the Lord Jesus ascended,
he promised to be with us always,
in the power of your Word and Holy Spirit.
On the night in which he gave himself up for us,
he took bread, gave thanks to you, broke the bread,
gave it to his disciples, and said:
"Take, eat; this is my body which is given for you.
Do this in remembrance of me."

When the supper was over, he took the cup,
gave thanks to you, gave it to his disciples, and said:
"Drink from this, all of you;
this is my blood of the new covenant,
poured out for you and for many
for the forgiveness of sins.
Do this, as often as you drink it,
in remembrance of me."

And so,
in remembrance of these your mighty acts in Jesus Christ,
we offer ourselves in praise and thanksgiving
as a holy and living sacrifice,

in union with Christ's offering for us,
as we proclaim the mystery of faith.

Christ has died; Christ is risen; Christ will come again.

Pour out your Holy Spirit on us gathered here,
    and on these gifts of bread and wine.
Make them be for us the body and blood of Christ,
that we may be for the world the body of Christ,
    redeemed by his blood.
By your Spirit make us one with Christ,
    one with each other,
    and one in ministry to all the world,
until Christ comes in final victory
    and we feast at his heavenly banquet.

Through your Son Jesus Christ,
with the Holy Spirit in your holy church,
all honor and glory is yours, almighty Father,
now and forever.
Amen.

[After the congregation recites the Lord's Prayer, the
service continues with the breaking of the bread.]

BREAKING THE BREAD

The pastor breaks the bread in silence, or while saying:

Because there is one loaf,
we, who are many, are one body, for we all partake of the
one loaf.
The bread which we break is a sharing in the body of Christ.

The pastor lifts the cup in silence, or while saying:

The cup over which we give thanks is a sharing in the
blood of Christ.

GIVING THE BREAD AND CUP

*The bread and wine are given to the people, with these or
other words being exchanged:*

The body of Christ, given for you. **Amen.**
The blood of Christ, given for you. **Amen.**

*The congregation may sing hymns while the bread and cup
are given.*

When all have received, the Lord's table is put in order.

The following prayer is then offered by the pastor or by all:

**Eternal God, we give you thanks for this holy mystery
in which you have given yourself to us.**

Grant that we may go into the world
in the strength of your Spirit,
to give ourselves for others,
in the name of Jesus Christ our Lord.
Amen.

Christ the Lord Is Risen Today

A beloved hymn by Charles Wesley, written in 1739 (*The United Methodist Hymnal,* p. 302)

Christ the Lord is risen today, Alleluia!
Earth and heaven in chorus say, Alleluia!
Raise your joys and triumphs high, Alleluia!
Sing, ye heavens, and earth reply, Alleluia!

Love's redeeming work is done, Alleluia!
Fought the fight, the battle won, Alleluia!
Death in vain forbids him rise, Alleluia!
Christ has opened paradise, Alleluia!

Lives again our glorious King, Alleluia!
Where, O death, is now thy sting? Alleluia!
Once he died our souls to save, Alleluia!
Where's thy victory, boasting grave? Alleluia!

Soar we now where Christ has led, Alleluia!
Following our exalted Head, Alleluia!

Made like him, like him we rise, Alleluia!
Ours the cross, the grave, the skies, Alleluia!

Hail the Lord of earth and heaven, Alleluia!
Praise to thee by both be given, Alleluia!
Thee we greet triumphant now, Alleluia!
Hail the Resurrection, thou, Alleluia!

King of glory, soul of bliss, Alleluia!
Everlasting life is this, Alleluia!
Thee to know, thy power to prove, Alleluia!
Thus to sing, and thus to love, Alleluia!

A Heart Strangely Warmed

From the journal of John Wesley, May 24, 1738:

In the evening I went very unwillingly to a society in Aldersgate Street, where one was reading Luther's preface to the Epistle to the Romans. About a quarter before nine, while he was describing the change which God works in the heart through faith in Christ, I felt my heart strangely warmed. I felt I did trust in Christ, Christ alone, for salvation; and an assurance was given me that He had taken away my sins, even mine, and saved me from the law of sin and death.

The General Rules of The Methodist Church

From *The Book of Discipline*, ¶104, pp. 78–80 (originally published in 1808, amended in 1848 and 1868).

There is only one condition previously required of those who desire admission into these societies: "a desire to flee from the wrath to come, and to be saved from their sins." But wherever this is really fixed in the soul it will be shown by its fruits.

It is therefore expected of all who continue therein that they should continue to evidence their desire of salvation,

First: By doing no harm, by avoiding evil of every kind, especially that which is most generally practiced, such as:

The taking of the name of God in vain.

The profaning the day of the Lord, either by doing ordinary work therein or by buying or selling.

Drunkenness: buying or selling spirituous liquors, or drinking them, unless in cases of extreme necessity.

Slaveholding; buying or selling slaves.

Fighting, quarreling, brawling, brother going to law with brother; returning evil for evil, or railing for railing; the using many words in buying or selling.

The buying or selling goods that have not paid the duty.

The giving or taking things on usury—i.e., unlawful interest.

Uncharitable or unprofitable conversation; particularly speaking evil of magistrates or of ministers.

Doing to others as we would not they should do unto us.

Doing what we know is not for the glory of God, as:

The putting on of gold and costly apparel.

The taking such diversions as cannot be used in the name of the Lord Jesus.

The singing those songs, or reading those books, which do not tend to the knowledge or love of God.

Softness and needless self-indulgence.

Laying up treasure upon earth.

Borrowing without a probability of paying; or taking up goods without a probability of paying for them.

It is expected of all who continue in these societies that they should continue to evidence their desire of salvation,

Secondly: By doing good; by being in every kind merciful after their power; as they have opportunity, doing good of every possible sort, and, as far as possible, to all men:

To their bodies, of the ability which God giveth, by giving food to the hungry, by clothing the naked, by visiting or helping them that are sick or in prison.

To their souls, by instructing, reproving, or exhorting all we have any intercourse with; trampling under foot that enthusiastic doctrine that "we are not to do good unless *our hearts be free to it.*"

By doing good, especially to them that are of the household of faith or groaning so to be; employing them preferably to others;

buying one of another, helping each other in business, and so much the more because the world will love its own and them only.

By all possible diligence and frugality, that the gospel be not blamed.

By running with patience the race which is set before them, denying themselves, and taking up their cross daily; submitting to bear the reproach of Christ, to be as the filth and offscouring of the world; and looking that men should say all manner of evil of them *falsely*, for the Lord's sake.

It is expected of all who desire to continue in these societies that they should continue to evidence their desire of salvation,

Thirdly: By attending upon all the ordinances of God; such are:

The public worship of God.

The ministry of the Word, either read or expounded.

The Supper of the Lord.

Family and private prayer.

Searching the Scriptures.

Fasting or abstinence.

These are the General Rules of our societies; all of which we are taught of God to observe, even in his written Word, which is the only rule, and the sufficient rule, both of our faith and practice. And all these we know his Spirit writes on truly awakened hearts. If there be any among us who observe them not, who habitually break any of them, let it be known unto them who watch over that soul as they who must give an account. We will admonish him of the error of his ways. We will bear with him for a season. But then, if he repent not, he hath no more place among us. We have delivered our own souls.